# The Funny Travel List Texas: 103 Slang Words, Texas Speak, and Sayin's

---

A Comical Language Dictionary of the Lone Star State

Chuck Acts

# Contents

# A Special Gift To Our Readers

Included in your purchase of this book, we are giving you a fun information book on Texas Slang, Sayings and the History of where they come from. We hope that you like it!

Click on the link below and let us know which email address to deliver it to:

www.funnytravellist.com

# Enjoy this book?

Honest reviews of my books are the only thing that helps bring attention of my books to other readers. I don't have the money to throw at advertising. Not yet anyway. So, If you enjoyed this book, I would be grateful if you could spend just 3 minutes leaving a review (It can be as short as you like).

The review button is on the upper left corner of our website. Just scan the code above and look upper left. - Thank you very much.

# Facebook Group

## WELCOME TO THE GATHERING!

---

If you want to get even more informative insight on Funny Travel Lists, you can always join our Facebook group. Our group includes: Travelers, Boon Dockers, Campers, RV Enthusiast, New Texans and Adventurers. This group was set up to discuss exploring funny and unique places and tell the stories of what we have come across in the US. We are a tight community seeking additional secret adventures while sharing some of our success and failures out on the road. We discuss all types of subjects and many that the general public are unaware! Stop by and see if we have a Funny Travel List book for your state! Be nice and share in the spirit of helping!

# The Funny Travel List Group

www.facebook.com/groups/funnytravellist/

Scan the QR code to easily get to the group

# The Origins of Texan Speak

---

*"Texas is a state of mind. Texas is an obsession. Above all, Texas is a nation in every sense of the word"*
***-John Steinbeck (Humphus, n.d.).***

What is Texas slang? Texas slang is a unique dialect that has been developed over time by the people who live in Texas. This dialect includes words and phrases that are not used in other parts of the country, and it can be difficult for outsiders to understand.

So, where does Texas slang come from? The origins of Texas slang can be traced back to the early 1800s when settlers from Texas began moving to other parts of the United States. These settlers brought their unique dialect with them, and it gradually began to spread.

Today, Texas slang is used by people throughout the state, and it continues to evolve over time. Some of the most common expressions include *"y'all," "fixin' to,"* and *"Howdy."*

Before *divin'* in, here are six steps to get *ya'll* started:

1. When *applyin'* Texan, think of words that end in 'g.'
2. Then, don't pronounce that 'g.'
3. Texans love it when you sprinkle the term *"fixin' to"* into dialogue.
4. Don't say "you guys." Refer to *'em* as *"ya'll."*

5. Don't ever call a Coca-Cola a 'pop;' They've got no idea what *ya'll talkin'* about.

6. Congratulations, *ya'll* now versed in Texan speak.

If you're visiting Texas, be sure to brush up on your Texas slang! It will help you to communicate with the locals and get a better understanding of their culture. Happy travels!

# Chapter 1:
# Texas Slang Words (Say It With a Twaaaannng)

***Ah***

This is the Texan version of the word 'I.' It's produced by adding a long twang to the 'I.' Some examples include '*mah*' (my) and '*lahk*' (like).

***Ah'ite.***

It's the Texan version for the word 'alright.' One example of where it can be used is to provide an affirmative answer when being asked to do something instead of *sayin'* yes.

***Bald***

The Texas slang term for the word 'boiled.' It's prominent when referring to eggs, "*Would ya like some hardbaldeggs?*"

***Big'O***

Pronounced "*big-oh*," this is a shortened version of the two words 'big' and 'old.'

***Caw***

This is the Texan version of 'call' - as in making a phone call. It's typically used in conjunction with the word '*mah*' or '*may*' (meaning me). Put them together, and you've got *cawmay*.

### ***Corn-Fed***

*Nuttin'* to do with maize at all! But rather someone big in stature. This phrase can be used to describe a big boy on the football team.

### ***Double-Backboned***

*Ya'll* can use this term to describe a brave person.

### ***Dun***

When *ya'll* completely tired, broken, or desolate, is when this phrase is used. One example is *"I'm dun."*

### ***Gimme***

*Gimme* is a Texan portmanteau of the words "give me." One use case example includes *"Gimme sum lovin'."*

### ***Gonna***

A slang term used to say "going to" in Texan speak.

### ***In'thang***

The Texan way to any 'anything.'

### ***Jeetjet***

It's no secret that food is a significant factor in Texas. So if you want to invite some people to a restaurant, you could ask *"Have ya'll jeetjet?"*

### ***Kicker***

This is used for the most compelling reason of pointing something out during an argument or conversation. For example: *"He cheated on her, but here's the kicker…."*

***Libel'ta***

A phrase used to express the liability of *havin'* to get *sumpin* (something) done. For example, *"She's libel'ta go out and have fun, now that she's single."*

***N***

This is the Texan way when saying '*than*.' It's predominantly used after a descriptive, such as *"Teacher was madder 'n a wet hen today."*

***Nuttin'***

The Lone Star state's way of saying 'nothing.' Meaning the word is used in cases such as *"He's got nuttin' on ya."*

***O'***

This Texan article is placed before the typical English articles 'a' and 'the.' It can be applied to animals and humans. One example includes *"Who's 0' good boy?"*

***Ov'air***

This is how the people in Texas say "over there." For example: *"Where's Scooter gone to now?" "He's ov'air in the barn."*

***Piddlee'o***

Texans use this phrase to refer to something or someone small. For example, *"That piglet is a piddlee'o thang."*

***Place***

This phrase is used when *referrin'* to a parcel of property. One example includes *"She's ov'air at Mcdonald place."*

***Purt/Purtee***

Texans use this slang word to describe *sumpin* as 'pretty' like *'em* other English folks.

***R***

Use this one on the slight side of caution. Even though pronounced as 'are,' Texans use it as a shortened version for the word 'our.'

***Show Nuff***

The shortened Texan version of the phrase "sure enough."

***Squeat***

This slang word is used to shorten the phrase "Let's go eat."

***Sumpin***

*Show nuff* by now *ya'll* know this one. But in case *ya* missed it, it's the Texan word for 'something.'

***Swate***

This is the Texan way of *sayin'* 'sweet.' One use case example includes: "Did *ya'll* say tomorrow's *meetin'* is canceled. *Swate*."

***Tak'n'ta***

Yep folks, when there's the need for a family *meetin'*, *ya'll* can say, *"I need to give that boy a tak'n'ta*." It's primarily used when *ya* need to have a stern word with someone.

***Thang***

This is another one of the first words that'll get stuck in *ya'lls* minds when *attemptin'* to speak Texan. It's their way of *sayin'* 'thing.'

***Up'dee***

This phrase means being 'insolate' or 'uppity' towards someone. One example of where ya'll can use it includes: *"Pete is being very up'dee with the manager lately."*

***Var'mit***

This word plays an integral part amongst hunters in Texas. It's used when small animal *huntin'* takes place. For example, *"Tommy and I went var'mit huntin' this morning."*

***Wat'nit***

This is the way that Texans say, "wasn't it."

***Whole'nuther***

A Texan term used when one wants to say "a whole other."

***Worsh***

The Texan word for 'wash.'

***Ya'll***

It's probably the most famous of all Texas slang terms, provided it's used correctly. It's used to address a group of folks and is the southern contraction of "you all."

***Yankee***

Texans use this word to refer to any individual originating from the north side of the Red River.

***Yer***

The way people from Texas say 'your.'

***Yonder***

Texans use this term to indicate that a person is at another location than they are. For example: "Where's Fort Worth?" "It's yonder in North Texas."

# Chapter 2:
# Texas *Sayin's*

---

***A Fur Piece***

Said when *sumpin's* far away, or to indicate a long distance.

***All Git Out***

A great way to convey that *sumpin* was good or done to the extreme! It can be used to say, *"I went to Blake's house, and his toys were all git out!"*

***All Hat, No Cattle***

Yep, this one's easy! This is used by a boastful person when they don't really have *anythin'* to brag about anyhow. It's like *talkin'* the talk and not *walkin'* the walk.

***"Bless Your Heart"***

This phrase is used two-fold. Firstly, you use it to display empathy in a bad situation, and it's also used sarcastically - especially between the ladies.

***Bright as a New Penny***

Texans use this phrase to describe an intelligent or clever person.

***Buzzard Bait***

Said of someone or *sumpin* that has died.

***Callin' Hogs all Night***

A phrase to describe a person or persons that are loud and noisy.

***Carryin' Brains in a Pocket***

A not-so-nice way to say someone is dumb.

***Cattywampus to Miss Jones'***

Someone from Texas will use this phrase as a means to say they're confused.

***Chin Musician***

A Texan term that refers to a talkative person.

***"Come Hell or High Water"***

This *sayin'* is used when it means that *sumpin'* will be done no matter the cost or what it takes. When a Texan says this, you can be assured of their loyalty.

***Cut up Like a Boardin'house Pit***

This is said of a person in Texas that is very nervous.

***"Dad Gum It"***

This is a nice way to replace any swear words when the situation is so dire; Ya'll don't have time to tell the kids to put them earmuffs on.

***"Don't Get Ya Panties in a Wad"***

This is one way of saying to someone to be more patient.

***"Don't Tip Over the Outhouse"***

A term used to tell a Texan to be careful or cautious.

### *Drier 'n Popcorn Fart*

A phrase that can be used when the lands are very dry before the rains have *fallin'*, or someone with a very dry sense of humor.

### *Eatin' Fried Chicken all Week Long*

Someone that is financially wealthy.

### *Expectin' Spoon-Feedin'*

A term used to describe someone that is vain in Texas.

### *Fair to Middlin'*

Texans say this when feeling happy and/or good about themselves or a situation they're in.

### *Flat as a Fritter*

A term used to describe a lean or petite person.

### *First Cousin to Moses Rose*

This term is used to describe someone who is shy or timid.

### *Get/Got on at*

This is the Texan phrase for when one has gained employment. It can be used as follows: *"Jesse, got on at Burger King yesterday."*

### *"Go Cork Yer Pistol"*

A nasty comeback used in Texan speak.

### *Got Caught in His/Her/Their Own Loop*

Someone from Texas will use this phrase to imply they've failed at *sumpin*.

***Hang Out the Washin'***

Said of something or someone that is strong, solid, or robust.

***Headin' for the Wagon Yard***

A phrase used to say goodbye to someone or announce departure in a conversation.

***Hog-Killin' Weather***

Texans say this when it's very cold outside.

***Hollerin' Down a Well***

The Texan way of telling someone that they're wasting time.

***Hopper's Busted***

Being said of someone that has taken ill.

***Hotter 'n Stolen Tamale***

This can be said of either the weather or someone that is very good *lookin'*.

***Huggin' a Rose Bush***

When *sumpin's* deemed as being unacceptable.

***"I Could Sit Still for That"***

*Meanin' sumpin's* acceptable to ya.

***"I Wasn't Born in Texas, but I Got Here as Fast as I Could"***

This is a popular Texas bumper sticker. It means you aren't a Texan native. But that *ya'll* live and breathe every moment Texan-style nonetheless.

### *"Jumped on Me, Like White on Rice"*

A Texan phrase used to say someone is very fast, especially if *ya'll* haven't seen them *comin'*.

### *Just Fell Off a Turnip/Watermelon/Tater Truck*

A term Texans use to refer to an unsophisticated person.

### *"Know When to Fold 'em"*

Yep, a line from the popular Kenny Rogers song, "The Gambler," but it also means that *ya'll* need to know when to call it quits and walk away from a situation or a person.

### *"Let's Chew the Rag"*

Texans use this term to greet someone or before the start of something that needs to be done.

### *Like a Blister*

Said of someone that is very lazy.

### *Lower Than a Gopher Hole*

This is used to describe someone that is feeling very sad.

### *Might Could*

Because *ev'thang* in Texas is *beeg*. The inhabitants of the Lone Star state like to add more words than needed. For instance, this phrase could be used as follows: *"We might could go to the mall today."*

### *Near About Past Going*

When *ya'll* hear someone *sayin'* this, it means they're very tired.

***No Hill for a Stepper***

Texans use this term to describe sumpin as being easy and requiring little to no effort.

***No Pot to Pee in or Window to Throw It Out of***

Used when describing someone poor or underprivileged.

***One Brick Shy of a Load***

Said of a person that is crazy.

***Out Where the Buses Don't Run***

Said of someone that is desolate and has no place to go.

***Ox in a Ditch***

This is a way of describing a problem one might have.

***Pantin' Like a Lizard on a Hot Rock***

This is said of someone that is very busy…with all *sorts'a thangs*.

***Pissin' up a Rope***

Texans use this term to describe a difficult task or situation.

***Pitch a Hissy Fit***

Mostly used when kids throw a tantrum. It's also used for adults when someone loses their shit *ish*.

***Raised on Concrete***

This term is used to describe someone that has been raised in the city or has moved there.

***Revolvin' Son of a Bitch***

A term used to describe a mean or bad person.

***Ridin' a Gravy Train With Biscuit Wheels***

Texans use this term to describe a person with a lot of luck.

***Sandpapered***

Texans would say this when they've been defeated by something or someone.

***Screwworm***

Said of an unwelcome person in Texas.

***Short Arms and Deep Pockets***

A Texas term used to describe a cheap or stingy person.

***Slicker 'n Slop Jar***

*Nuttin'* to do with someone *bein'* messy, but rather refers to a dishonest person.

***Sittin' on a Nest***

A way to describe a pregnant woman.

***Suckin' the Hind Teat***

Said of a useless or inept person or situation.

***"The Barn Door's Open and the Mule's Tryin' to Get Out"***

Lol! Probably one of the best ways to say the cucumber has left the salad, i.e., mate, ya fly is down!

***"The Only Hell His/Her Mama Ever Raised"***

A very Texan way of *sayin'* someone's real mad or argumentative. Also, a nicer way to say someone is hot-headed.

***"This Ain't My First Rodeo"***

When someone says this, they're tryin' to say that they are either capable or experienced in a matter.

***Throw Your Hat O'er the Windmill***

This is one Texan way to say it's time to celebrate.

***Tighter 'n Bark on a Log***

Texans use this term to describe a drunk or intoxicated person.

***"You Can Take That to the Bank"***

*Meanin'* something is true and can also be used to describe an honest person.

***Wide as Two Ax Handles***

Rude as it might be (to those in the know), this is one way of *sayin'* someone's overweight.

***Wilder 'n Acre of Snakes***

This phrase is used to describe a 'loose' or immoral person.

***Wouldn't Cut Hot Butter***

Someone or something very dull.

# A Special Gift To Our Readers

Included in your purchase of this book, we are giving you a fun information book on Texas Slang, Sayings and the History of where they come from. We hope that you like it!

Click on the link below and let us know which email address to deliver it to:

www.funnytravellist.com

# Enjoy this book?

Honest reviews of my books are the only thing that helps bring attention of my books to other readers. I don't have the money to throw at advertising. Not yet anyway. So, If you enjoyed this book, I would be grateful if you could spend just 3 minutes leaving a review (It can be as short as you like).

The review button is on the upper left corner of our website. Just scan the code above and look upper left. - Thank you very much.

# Facebook Group

## WELCOME TO THE GATHERING!

If you want to get even more informative insight on Funny Travel Lists, you can always join our Facebook group. Our group includes: Travelers, Boon Dockers, Campers, RV Enthusiast, New Texans and Adventurers. This group was set up to discuss exploring funny and unique places and tell the stories of what we have come across in the US. We are a tight community seeking additional secret adventures while sharing some of our success and failures out on the road. We discuss all types of subjects and many that the general public are unaware! Stop by and see if we have a Funny Travel List book for your state! Be nice and share in the spirit of helping!

# The Funny Travel List Group

www.facebook.com/groups/funnytravellist/

Scan the QR code to easily get to the group

# References

Dingus, A. (1994, December 1). *More colorful Texas sayings than you can shake a stick at.* TexasMonthly. https://www.texasmonthly.com/being-texan/more-colorful-texas-sayings-than-you-can-shake-a-stick-at/

Enchanting Texas. (2022, January 11). *28 famous Texas quotes and Texas sayings.* Enchanting Texas. https://enchantingtexas.com/texas-quotes-sayings/

Humphus, B. (n.d.). *15 Texas sayings ideas | Texas, Texas quotes, loving Texas.* Pinterest. https://za.pinterest.com/bhumphus/texas-sayings/

Norton, K. (n.d.). *30 things people from Texas have to explain to out-of-towners.* Movoto. https://www.movoto.com/guide/tx/things-people-from-texas-have-to-explain/

Ray, D. (n.d.). *Texas dialect | Words, Texas, phrase.* Pinterest. https://za.pinterest.com/pin/AcJ1ho2z14UUJlaGw9NohNLDVSsOoGaDqpufifXgmCFq-p6FxeuBAeE/

UStravelia. (2014, December 22). *118 famous Texas sayings and phrases along with their meanings.* UStravelia. https://ustravelia.com/famous-texas-sayings-phrases

Made in the USA
Coppell, TX
03 May 2024

31985237R00015